FLIPMAN® Rules!

Let's DO Well!

Terry Hawkins

Copyright © Terry Hawkins 2014

First published 2011

Copyright remains the property of the author and apart from any fair dealing for the purposes of private study, research, criticism or review, as permitted under the Copyright Act, no part may be reproduced by any process without written permission.

All inquiries should be made to;

Terry Hawkins
PO Box #512, 1601 N Sepulveda Boulevard
Manhattan Beach CA 90266

Phone: +1 (310) 937-1183
Email: Terry@TerryHawkins.com
Website: www.TerryHawkins.com

Cover design and typesetting: Think Productions

National Library of Australia Cataloguing-in-Publication entry

Author: Hawkins, Terry L.

Title: Let's DO Well / Terry L. Hawkins.

ISBN: 9780987057433 (pbk.)

Series: Hawkins, Terry L. Flipman Rules!

Target Audience: For primary school children.

Subjects: Chronic diseases in children--Psychological aspects--Juvenile literature. Chronic diseases--Psychological aspects--Juvenile literature. Chronically ill children--Psychological aspects--Juvenile literature. Chronically ill--Psychological aspects--Juvenile literature.

Dewey Number: 362.19892

For more information on Terry Hawkins and her other products please visit

www.TerryHawkins.com

Illustrations: Mick Tate

www.micktate.com

Let's DO Well!

written by Terry Hawkins

BIG SKY PUBLISHING
www.bigskypublishing.com.au

FLIPMAN and PITMAN are registered trademarks of Terry Hawkins. © 2014 Terry Hawkins

Acknowledgements

Let's **DO** *Well!* would never have become a reality if it were not for the passion and commitment of a very special man, Gary Bertwistle (co-founder of Australia's leading cycling foundation "Tour de Cure" and "6 Strings 4 Cancer"). Gary, your absolute desire to give children a resource that helps them live a healthy lifestyle is what made this book possible. You are a legend in your own right and I salute you and the entire Tour de Cure crew – Go Flipman!

To Charley Bertwistle – WOW! What a special girl you are! Thank you for your amazing input into how a child perceives this illness. Your insights gave that much needed clarity that only a child can give. You are such a Flipgirl!!

To Mick Tate! Well Mick, you have done it again. Thank you for adding your special magic to make *Let's* **DO** *Well!* such an engaging book through your incredible illustrations.

Dedication

Cancer – the word alone can sound frightening to many adults, so how do we explain it to a child? How do we answer those challenging questions when a loved one, special friend or even a child's classmate is diagnosed with such a serious illness?

My own father passed away at the very young age of 48 from lung cancer, when I was 15 years old. Our family found it very difficult to fathom, especially my younger sister and brother.

Let's **DO** *Well!* is dedicated to every person who has ever been affected by the tragic effects of this illness. The aim of this book is to offer you support and encouragement when facing one of life's most challenging moments.

May Flipman be with you always!

Chapter 1

Flipman was walking through the park when he noticed a small boy sitting on the grass with his skateboard in his hand.

All the other kids were having lots of fun playing, and squeals of laughter could be heard a mile away.

The sun was shining and the birds were chirping. Everyone seemed to be enjoying the summer sunshine.

Everyone, except for the little boy sitting on the grass. He looked very sad and alone.

Just at that moment, Flipman noticed Jack whizzing past.

"Hey Flipman!" he squealed with laughter. "Check this out." Jack sped past and leapt into the air with his skateboard.

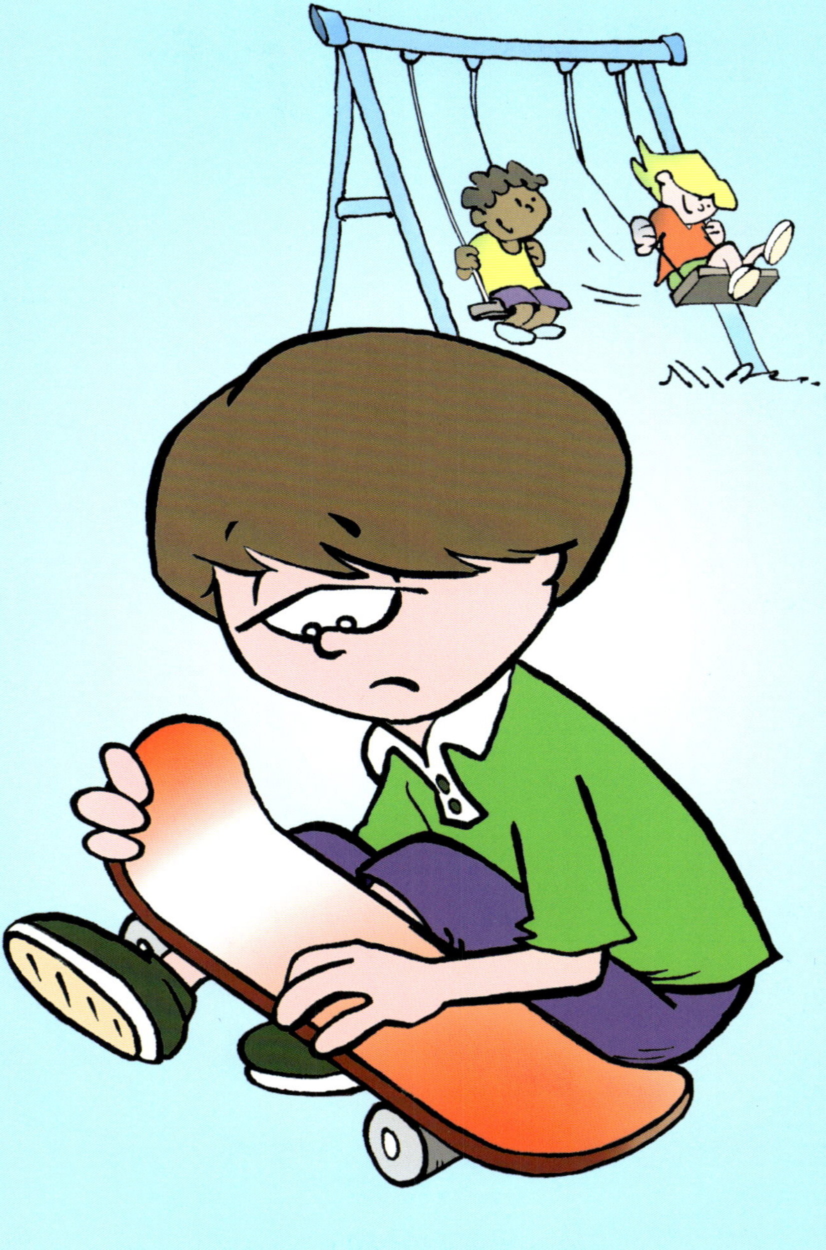

"That's called an Ollie," he said with pride as he smiled a smile that took up nearly his entire face.

"WOW Jack! I remember when you could hardly stand up on your skateboard. Now look at you, you're amazing. How did you get to be so good?" asked Flipman, very impressed by Jack's skating ability.

"You taught me, Flipman, that if we just stick at something and keep practicing over and over then we will get better and better.

"I was really bad at it in the beginning and almost gave up but each time I fell I would remember to say, 'Every day, in every way, I'm getting better and better'," said Jack proudly.

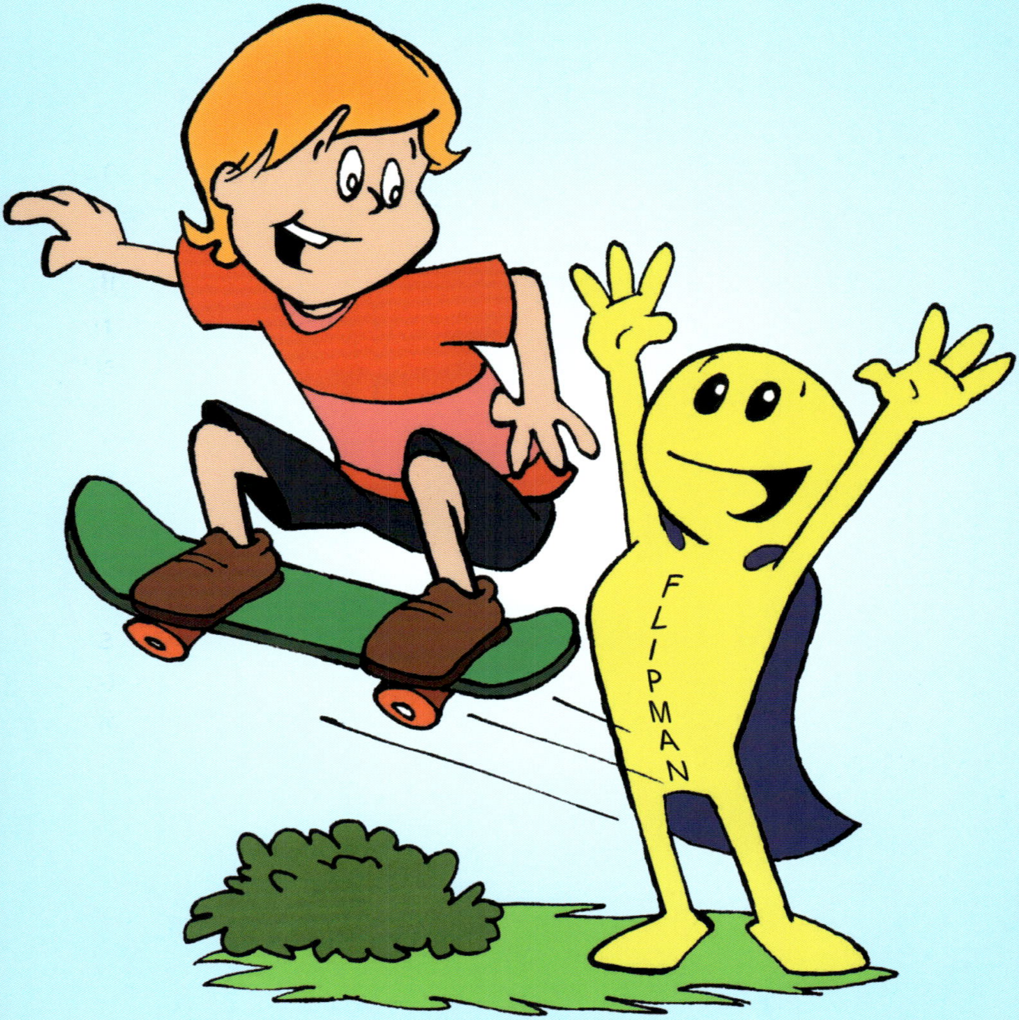
FLIPMAN

As they walked along together, Jack and Flipman came closer to the little boy sitting on the grass. "Do you know that little boy? He looks so sad," said Flipman.

"Yes I do. His name is Freddie and his Grandpa has cancer. He and his Grandpa are really close and he has been sad ever since he found out.

"You know Flipman, I think you might be able to help him. Come meet him with me," said Jack.

"Hi Freddie. I would love you to meet a very good friend of mine. This is Flipman," said Jack, watching as Freddie started to look very wary of this big yellow character in front of him.

"Hi Jack, nice to see you," said Freddie sounding very sad. "Who is your friend again?" he asked, looking very curious.

6

"This is Flipman. Flipman is the superhero that lives within us ... well, he can explain," laughed Jack as he smiled at Flipman.

"Hi Freddie. It's great to meet you. You seem very sad. What's up?" asked Flipman.

"My Mum said my Grandpa is very sick. He has cancer and is in hospital. I don't think he will get better because Mum said he is very old. I love him so much and it makes my heart hurt so bad when I think that he might die." Freddie started to cry.

"That must be so sad for you Freddie and it's important to let our feelings come out. Crying is our body's way of saying it's sad. It is so important to let it out rather than trying to keep it inside. You are very brave to allow yourself to cry," said Flipman.

8

"I get so confused Flipman. Sometimes I feel so many different feelings about Grandpa. I can feel sad, I can feel angry, I can feel like crying and sometimes I feel them all at the same time," said Freddie with a confused look on his face.

"You are so right Freddie. There are lots of feelings that can come up for us when someone we love is sick.

"It is normal and healthy to feel them all. Whether we feel scared, sad, angry, frustrated or upset, we need to remember that all of our feelings are important. Sometimes it can help to talk to someone we trust so they can support us. It can also help to learn more about this disease.

"Cancer can seem very scary and sometimes there are lots of things that we would like to ask but we don't know how or who to ask.

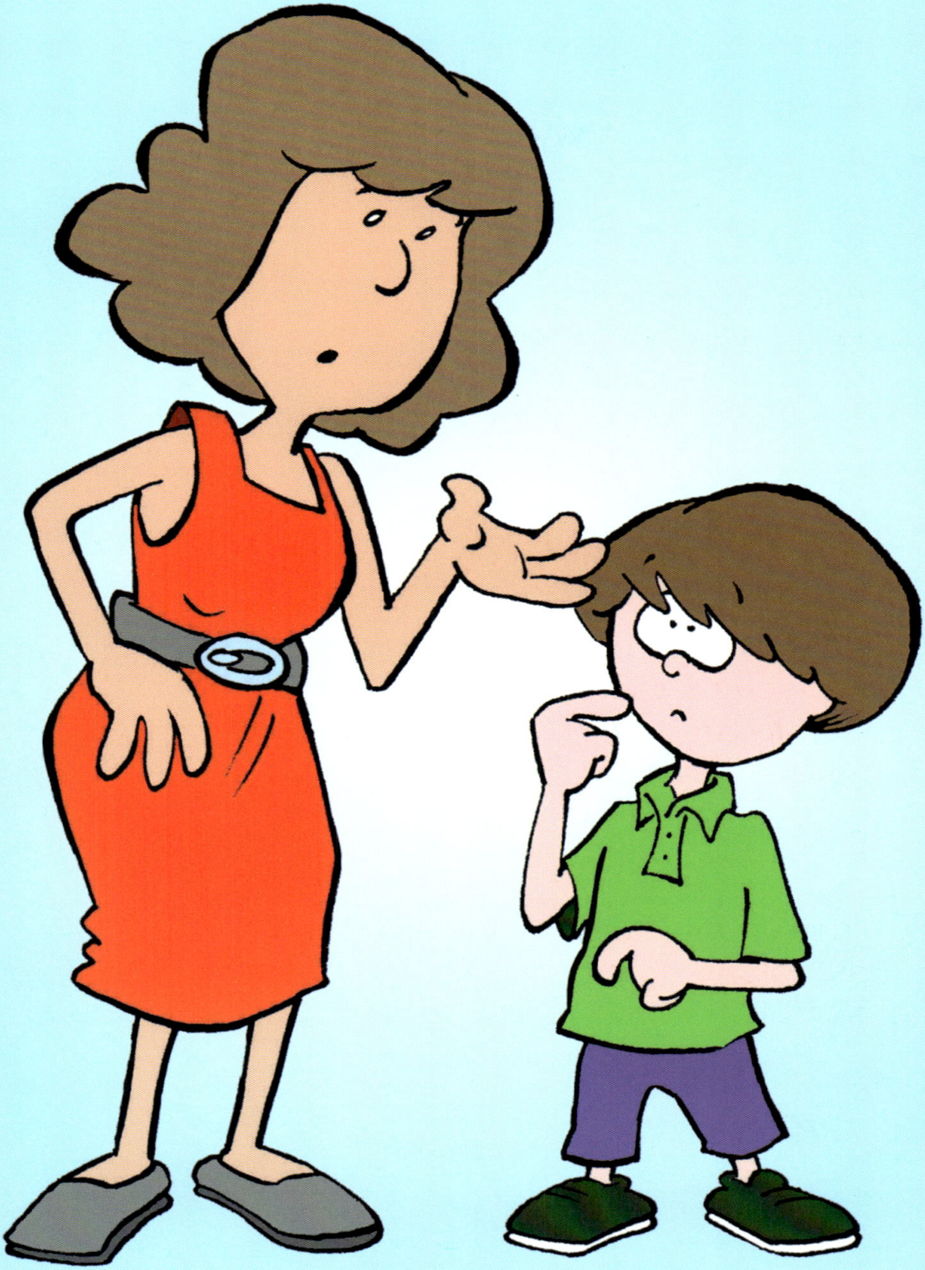

"Is there anything you want to ask me Freddie?" said Flipman, wanting to make sure that Freddie understood what cancer is and what it isn't.

"Well, there is actually. A girl at school told me her uncle had cancer and he died. Does everyone die from cancer?" asked Freddie looking very worried.

"No, of course not. There are lots of people who survive this illness and respond really well to treatment. They can go on to fully recover and live long and healthy lives. When people are older, though, it can be harder for their bodies to fight back. I can understand why this comment would have upset you Freddie.

"It's scary to think that someone we love might die and that's why it's so important to talk about it with people that can give you the right information."

12

Chapter 2

"Do you have any other questions Freddie?" asked Flipman.

Freddie nodded. "There is one more question I have, Flipman. One of the kids at school said that you could catch cancer when you spend time with someone who has it.

"Now I'm scared to go to the hospital and visit Grandpa but I miss him so much. I know he misses me too, but I don't want to catch it too and get sick," said Freddie feeling guilty for what he had just said.

"Oh Freddie, that must have been awful for you to hear and I am really proud of you for being so honest with me. I can imagine how sad that would make you feel.

"You and your Grandpa love each other so much that I'm sure both of you are feeling very sad and confused right now.

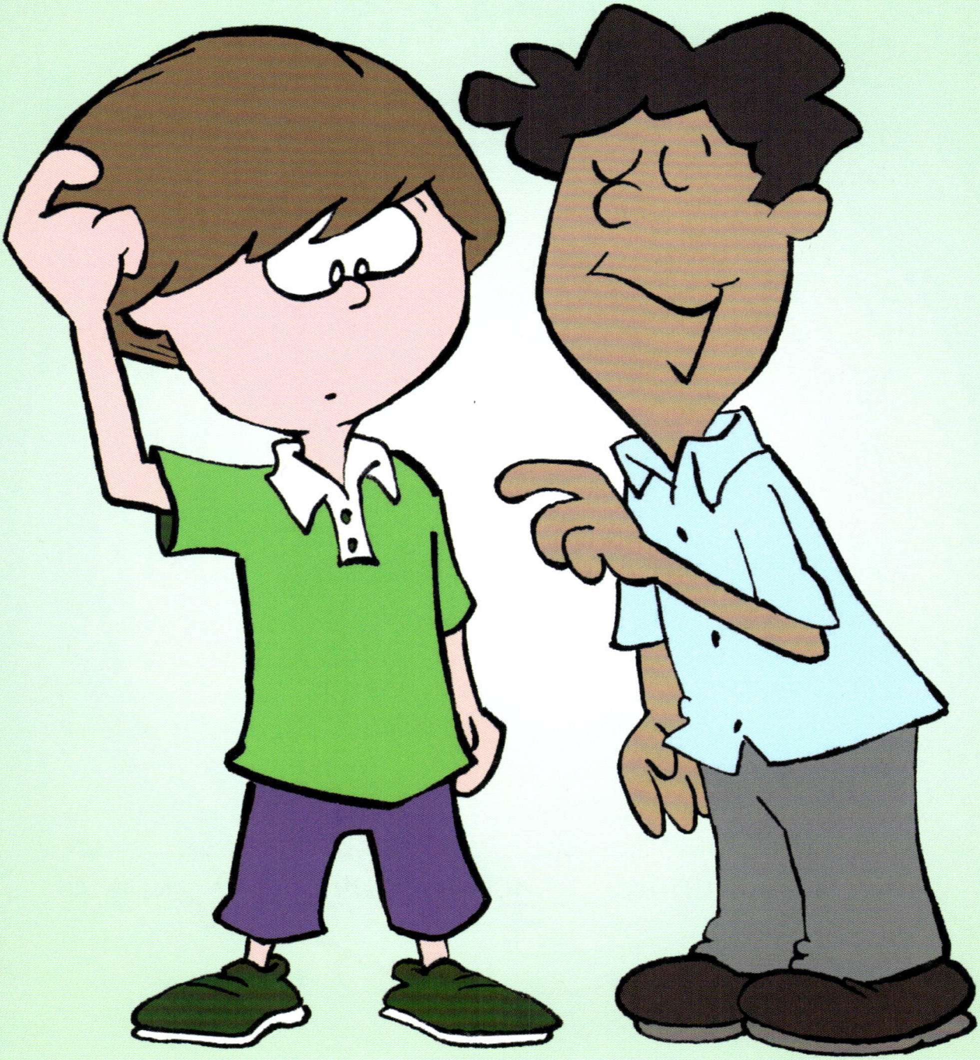

"You need to know, Freddie, that it is completely safe to hug and cuddle people who are dealing with cancer. In fact, they probably need lots of cuddles and loads of love as they deal with this very challenging time in their lives.

"It can also be hard to know what to say to the people we love when they are sick. Just like you, Freddie, some people shy away from visiting people who are sick, but this is when they need us the most.

"One of the reasons we get so scared, is because we don't really understand a lot about the illness.

"Cancer can seem like a scary word so it's important to understand what it is, what happens when someone we love gets sick with cancer and to learn about some of the words you may hear. Do you know what cancer is, Freddie?"

16

"No, I don't, Flipman, but I do know it's a very bad thing to get," said Freddie, looking frightened.

"It can be a scary disease, Freddie, especially if we don't know anything about it. Let me explain what I know.

"Our body is made up of a whole lot of little cells, billions and billions of them in fact. They are the shape of a little ball and are so small we can't even see them with our eyes.

When a whole lot of these cells join together, they make tissue and when you get a whole lot of tissue joining together, it makes up an organ. Organs help our body to work properly.

"Our lungs, our heart, our skin, our liver and our colon are just a few examples of the different organs in our body."

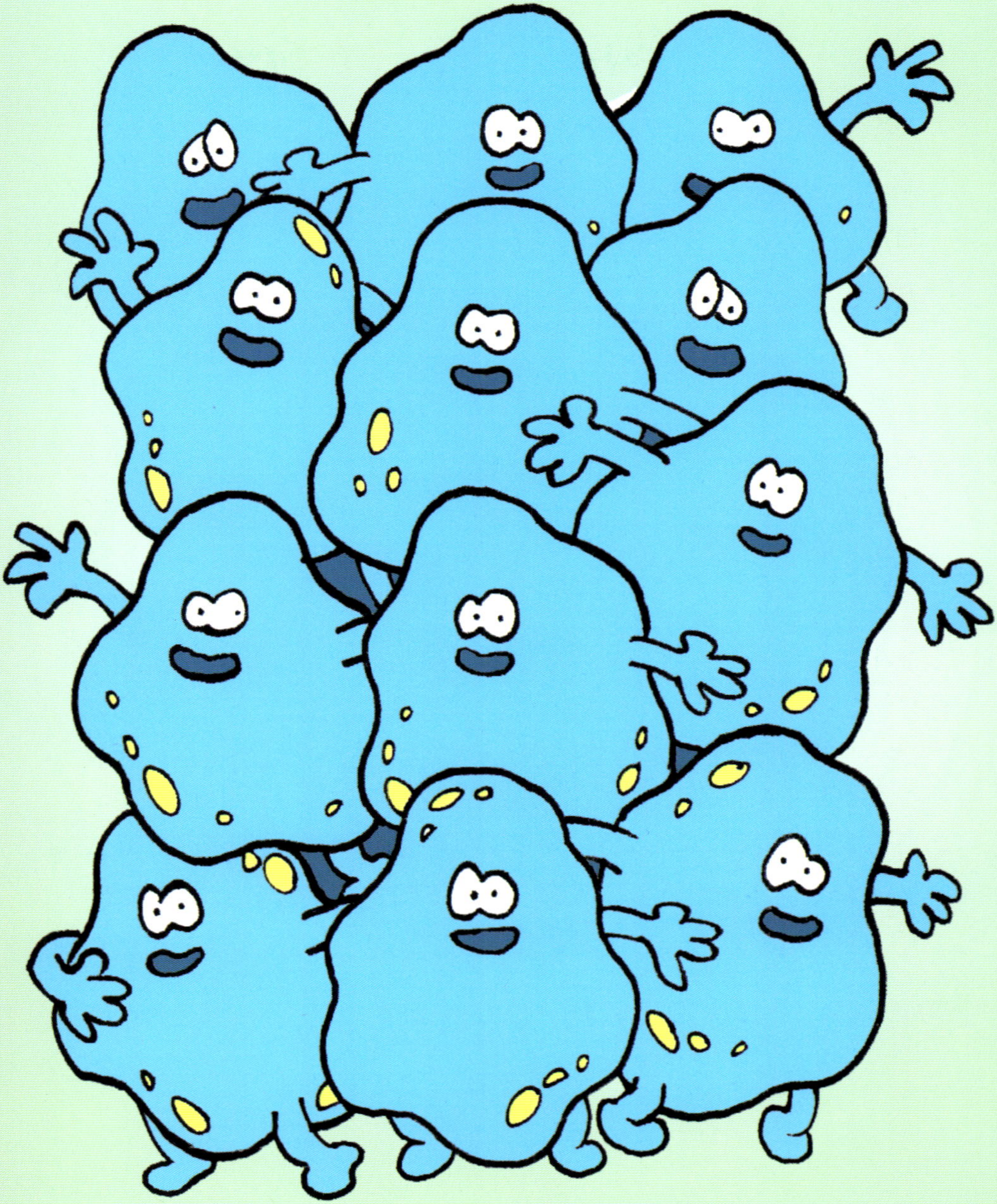

Flipman showed Freddie a picture showing the organs of the human body.

"These organs then help our body to run properly. They pump our blood; they help us to breathe and eat and to generally feel good.

"Sometimes our cells get sick and when enough of them get sick, then the tissue and the organ gets sick. That's when it's called cancer.

"As I said before, Freddie, not everybody who gets cancer dies. In fact, most people who get cancer survive, especially if it is discovered early. There are lots of different treatments for cancer. Some people choose something called radiation (ray-dee-ay-shun), some choose chemotherapy (kee-mo-ther-ar-pea) or both and other people can choose more natural therapies.

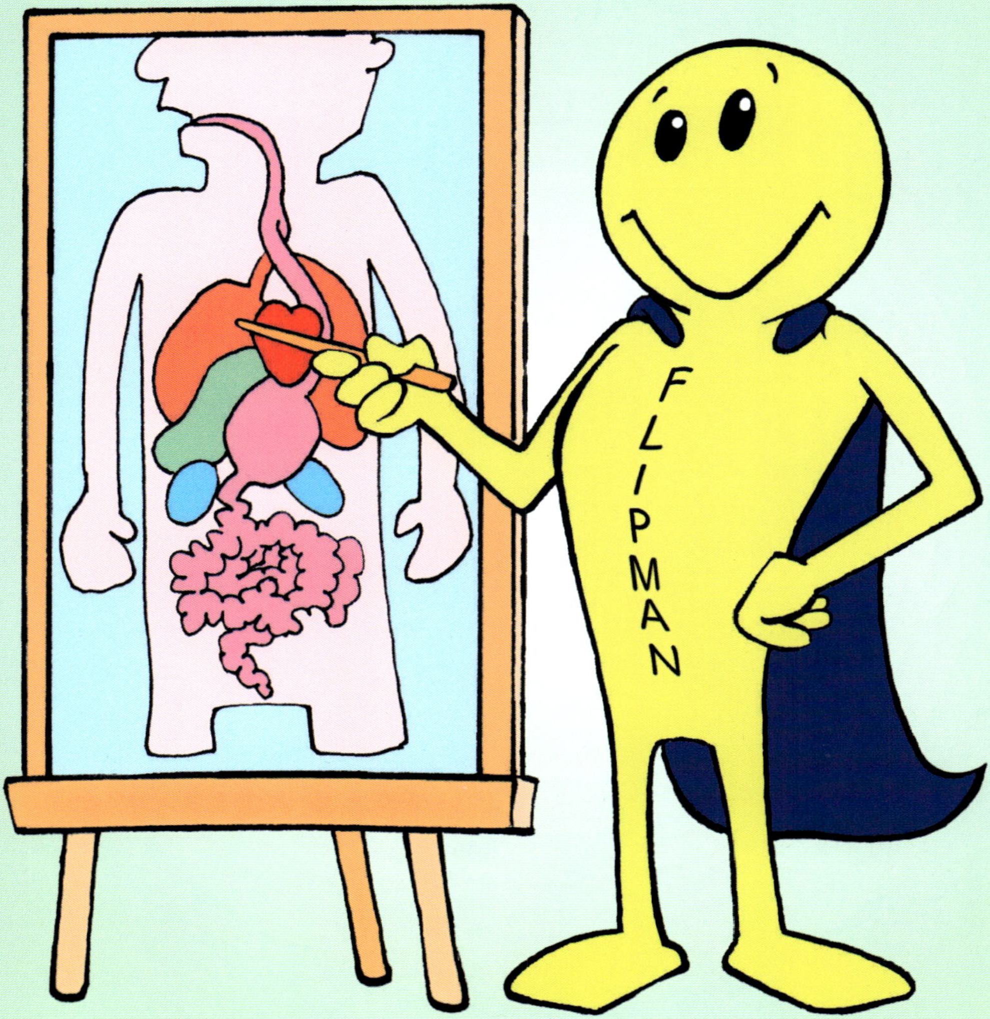
FLIPMAN

"Some of these treatments can seem scary. Chemotherapy is a liquid that is fed into the veins. It kills fast growing cells like cancer.

"Sometimes people's hair may fall out when they have chemotherapy, because hair is made from fast growing cells as well.

"Radiation is another scary word that you might hear. It is a type of treatment used to stop the sick cells in the body from growing or spreading.

"During treatment, a machine will send invisible rays to the sick cells in the person's body as they lie on a bed. They will not see or feel the radiation. Their job is to hold their body very still so that the invisible rays only go to the sick cells in their body."

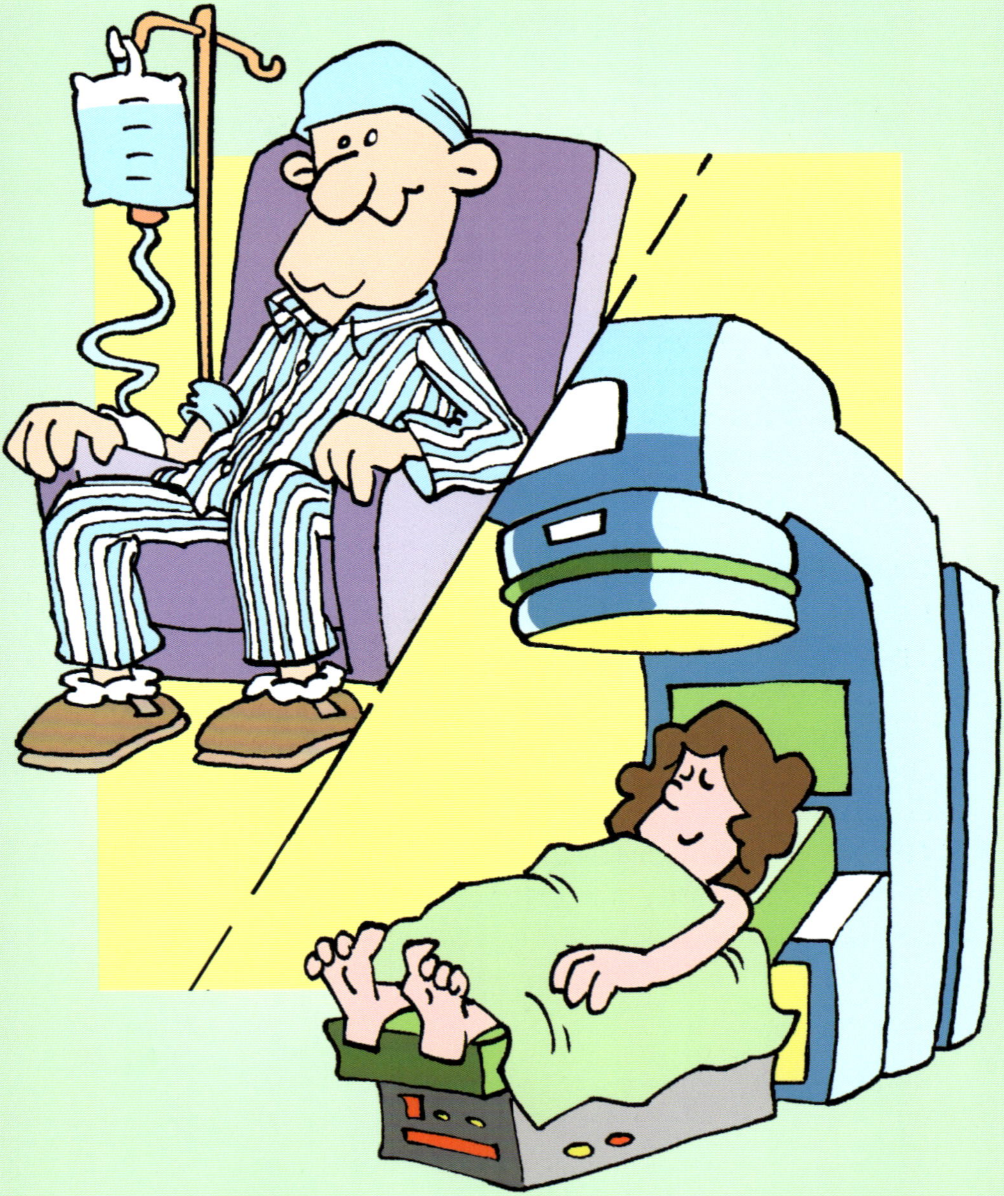

Chapter 3

Flipman was very proud of how well Freddie had listened.

"You are such a great listener, Freddie. Well done! I'll show you how to be brave so you can give your Grandpa lots of love and support, but for now here are a few ideas that might help you both to feel close when you can't be together.

"Why don't you write him some letters and tell him all the things you love about him and love doing with him. You could also draw pictures of the two of you playing, being happy and having fun, even tell him some jokes.

"I'm sure that would make him laugh. Laughter is such good medicine when we are feeling sick. When we laugh, our body produces endorphins (en-door-phins) to help make us feel better and help us fight disease. I like to call them 'Happy Helpers'.

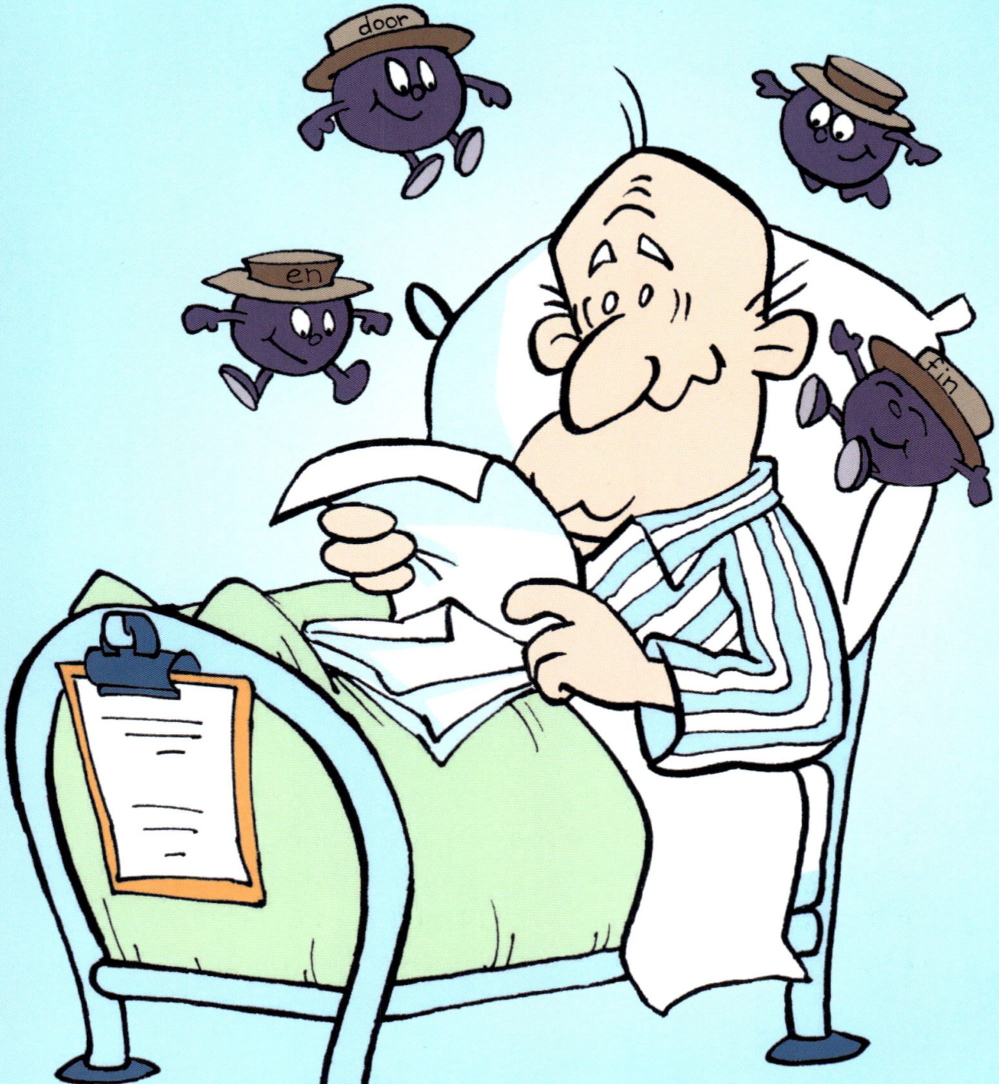
door
en
fin

"The most important thing you can do for your Grandpa, though, is to help him focus on being well even when he doesn't feel like it. That's when I can help. I can show him how to be a Flipman when he's feeling down," said Flipman.

"Flipman, would you come with me to visit Grandpa? I would feel so much better if you were with me, then Grandpa and I could learn about being Flipman together," said Freddie.

"I would love to, Freddie. It would be wonderful to meet your Grandpa," replied Flipman.

Flipman and Freddie went to visit Grandpa that afternoon. Flipman loved meeting Grandpa and hearing about all the adventures he and Freddie had been on. Lots of laughter could be heard coming from Grandpa's room.

26

As Flipman was leaving Grandpa's room, he noticed a young girl sitting on a hospital bed. She had no hair and a smile that would make anyone feel happy. "Well who are you then?" she asked with a big grin, as Flipman walked past.

"I'm Flipman and who are you?" asked Flipman with a smile.

"I'm Chloe. I love your blue cape. Are you some kind of superhero?"

"Yes, I am!" laughed Flipman. "I actually live within each and every one of us. I'm the part of us that is courageous, loving, honest and kind. I am in you and I help us to SEE, SAY, FEEL and DO things in a positive way.

"My job is to help you when you're feeling down and need a friend to lean on," explained Flipman.

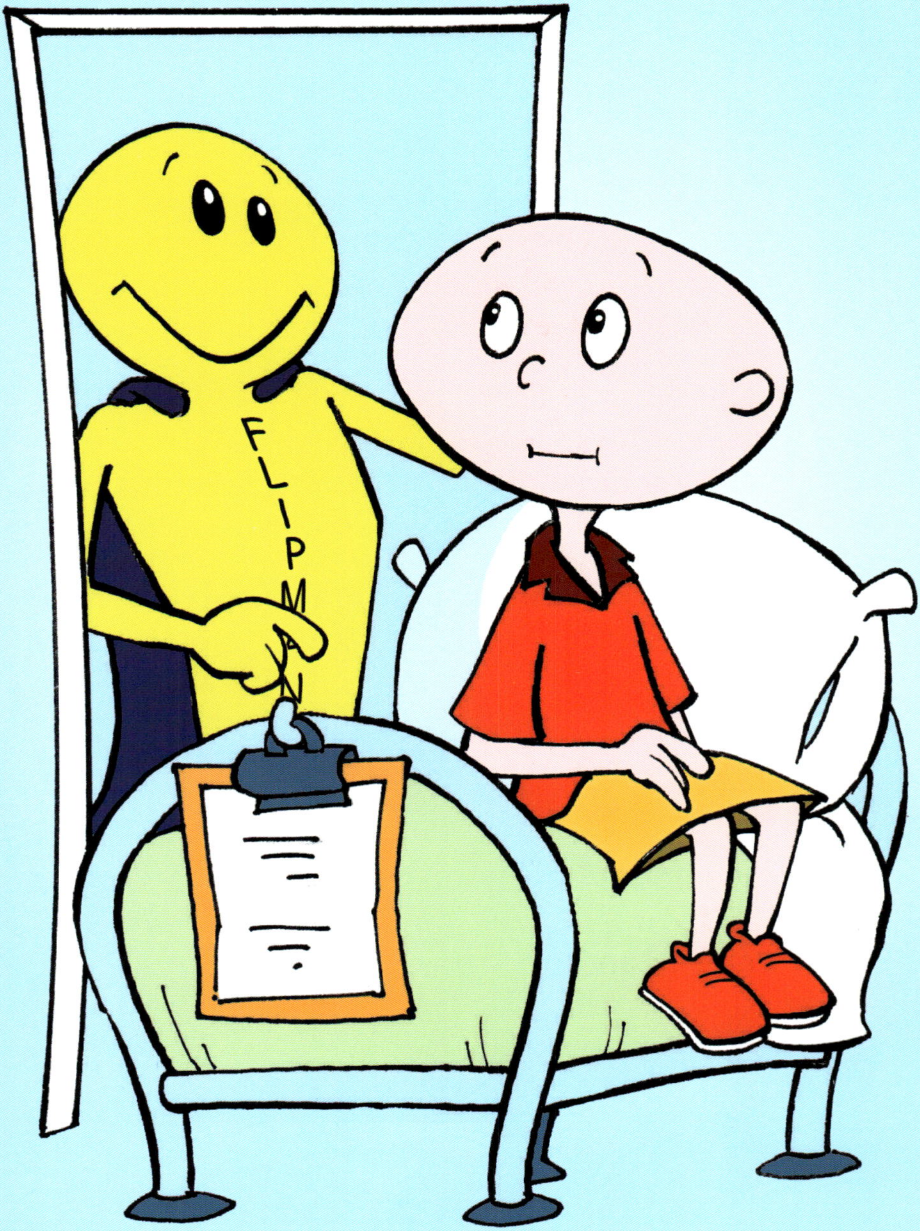
FLIPMAN

"Well I could use a friend like you right now, Flipman. I am having treatment for cancer and there are some days when I don't feel happy at all," said Chloe looking pleased that she had met Flipman.

"Sometimes I feel so tired and so sick that I couldn't care what I say or what I think or what I eat for that matter," said Chloe in a cranky voice.

"What a brave girl you are, Chloe. You are right that it can be really challenging to focus on being well when we feel so sick all of the time. That's what I am here for. I want to show you how you can give yourself the best possible support during this time that you're ill.

"The best thing we can do to help our body when it is ill is to make sure that everything we eat, think, feel, say and do are as positive as possible," explained Flipman.

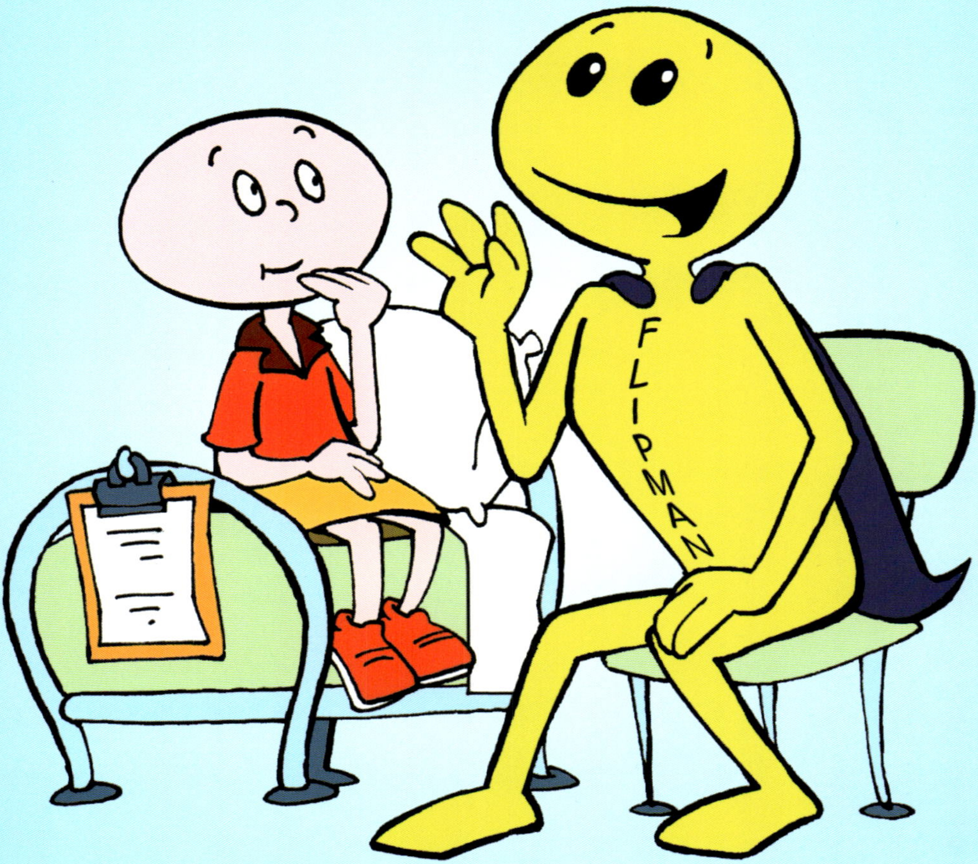
FLIPMAN

"So if I do all of these things, Flipman, will I be cured of the cancer?" asked Chloe.

"I wish I could answer that Chloe," said Flipman.

"What I can say is that if you do, you are helping your body to be as fit, healthy and happy as it can be. This can help get rid of the bad cells and make the good cells even stronger."

"But what if I don't feel like eating all the healthy foods, Flipman? Sometimes I feel like eating junk and I don't want to eat healthy all the time. How do I handle that, Flipman?"

Chloe continued, "I also feel really, really sad but I don't want to be sad all the time. I just can't help it.

32

Can you help me Flipman?" Chloe asked, looking worried.

"I know it can seem challenging at times, Chloe, and it can feel like we have no power to change how we feel," explained Flipman.

"I think I can help you Chloe. I'm your superhero and I live within you, right?" asked Flipman.

"Yes, you're right!" answered Chloe, with a big smile.

"So, every superhero you know always has to fight who?" asked Flipman.

"A villain!" Chloe squealed excitedly.

"That's right. Well done," said Flipman.

"We also have a villain that lives within us. His name is Pitman. Just as I am your superhero, Pitman is the villain."

34

Chapter 4

"Pitman is the part of us that teases us and tempts us to do all the things that don't help us to feel good."

"Like when I want to feel sorry for myself and eat all of the junky food," said Chloe.

"That's exactly what Pitman tempts us to do, Chloe. Well done again." Flipman was very impressed with Chloe's answers.

"But what if I can't stop Pitman?" asked Chloe, feeling more than a little worried.

"The most important thing," began Flipman, "is to listen to how we speak and think and feel. We also have to listen to the words we use because when we use negative words, it's like feeding Pitman.

Go on Chloe, eat all of the junk food. You know you want to
PITMAN

"He just gobbles up all the words that make us feel bad, making him stronger and we don't want that!

"Pitman loves words like:

I can't do this.

I'm no good.

I hate myself.

I'll never get better.

I hate everyone else.

I always make mistakes.

Nobody wants to be my friend.

It's all too hard.

Nobody likes me.

I'll never stop crying.

I'll never be happy again.

I'm not smart enough; fast enough; big enough; small enough; funny enough…

"The greatest thing of all, though, is that Flipman can **always** shrink Pitman if we want him to.

Mmmm, I love those words. I grow stronger and stronger. Now I'll really be able to push that Chloe around.

I can't do it, I'm no good This is too hard, I'll never be able to do this. Nobody likes me. I hate myself.

"Remember, Pitman and Flipman both live within us and we're in charge of both of them," Flipman continued.

"When we are changing from feeling miserable and sad to feeling happy and positive, we sometimes have to trick Pitman."

Chloe was now starting to feel excited. Maybe she could get rid of Pitman and stop feeling miserable.

"So how do I do that, Flipman?" she asked.

Flipman smiled.

"Sometimes when you don't feel like doing something you can pretend. That way you can trick your brain," smiled Flipman as Chloe nodded.

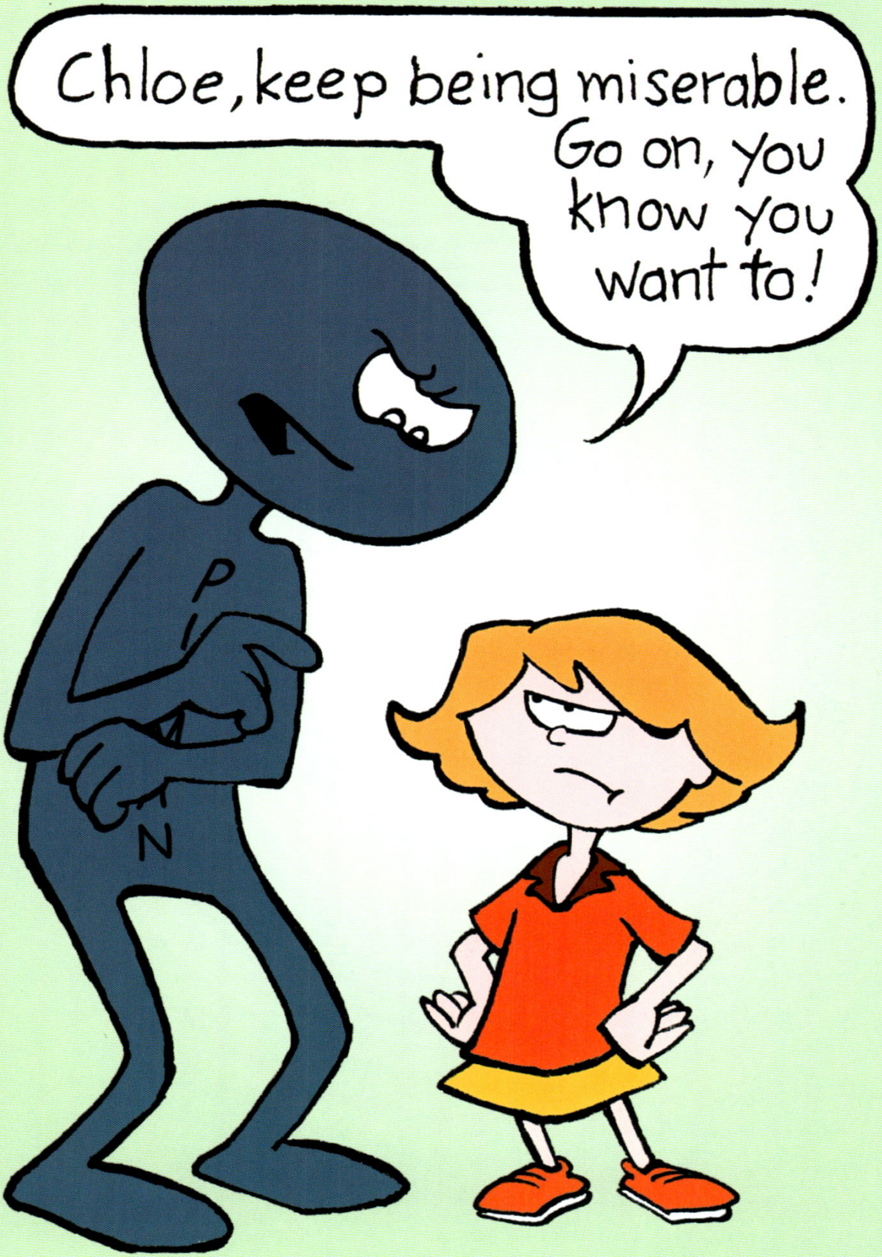
Chloe, keep being miserable. Go on, you know you want to!

"When we get that funny feeling or hear that voice inside that starts telling us that everything is awful and to only look at all the bad things, that's really Pitman being sneaky. He has snuck inside our head and is teasing us. He's saying, 'Go on Chloe, keep being miserable'."

"When we get that feeling and hear Pitman, we have to be really strong. That's when you call on me, I'll help you.

"In a really loud voice we'll say,

GO AWAY Pitman!

I AM happy, healthy and positive!

I AM happy, healthy and positive!

I AM happy, healthy and positive!"

Chloe looked very worried all of a sudden. "Does that mean I'm never allowed to feel sad or angry again Flipman?" she asked.

I am happy, healthy and positive, I am happy, healthy and positive

"No, not at all," laughed Flipman. "Remember, I said that it is really important to feel all of our feelings, but we don't need to stay stuck in those feelings.

"That's the difference, Chloe. We decide how long we stay sad or angry. We control our feelings.

"But sometimes when we are ready to feel happy again, Pitman will still try to pull us down into his PIT of Misery to keep us sad or angry.

"He loves it when we go down into the PIT with him. He has a PIT party with all of his PIT pals! We all go to the PIT sometimes and that's why it is so important to call on the Flipman within you, when you need to.

"So let's check to make sure your Flipman is working for you, Chloe.

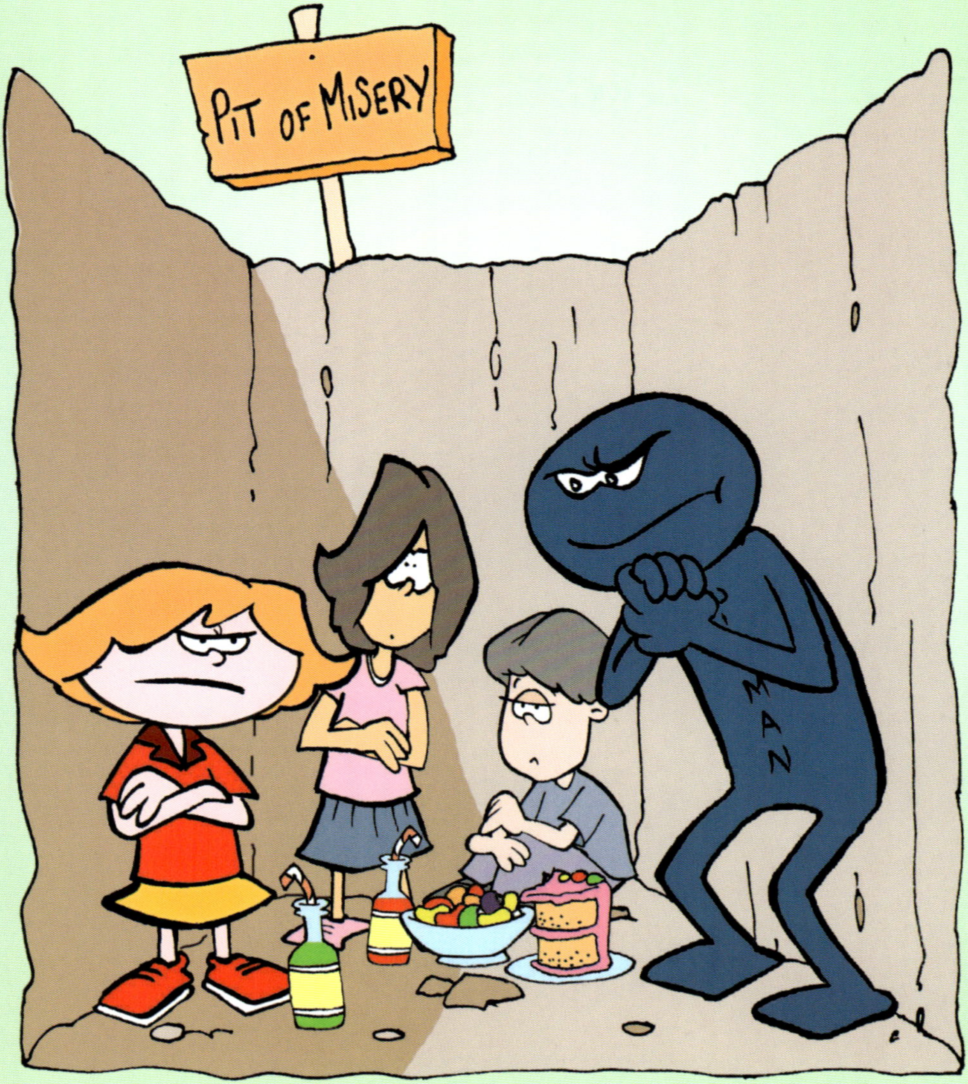
PIT OF MISERY
MAN

"Can you SEE yourself feeling happy again?" Flipman asked.

"Yes I can," she said.

"Can you **MAKE A PICTURE** in your mind of what you look like when you're happy, healthy and positive, Chloe?"

"Yes I can, Flipman!"

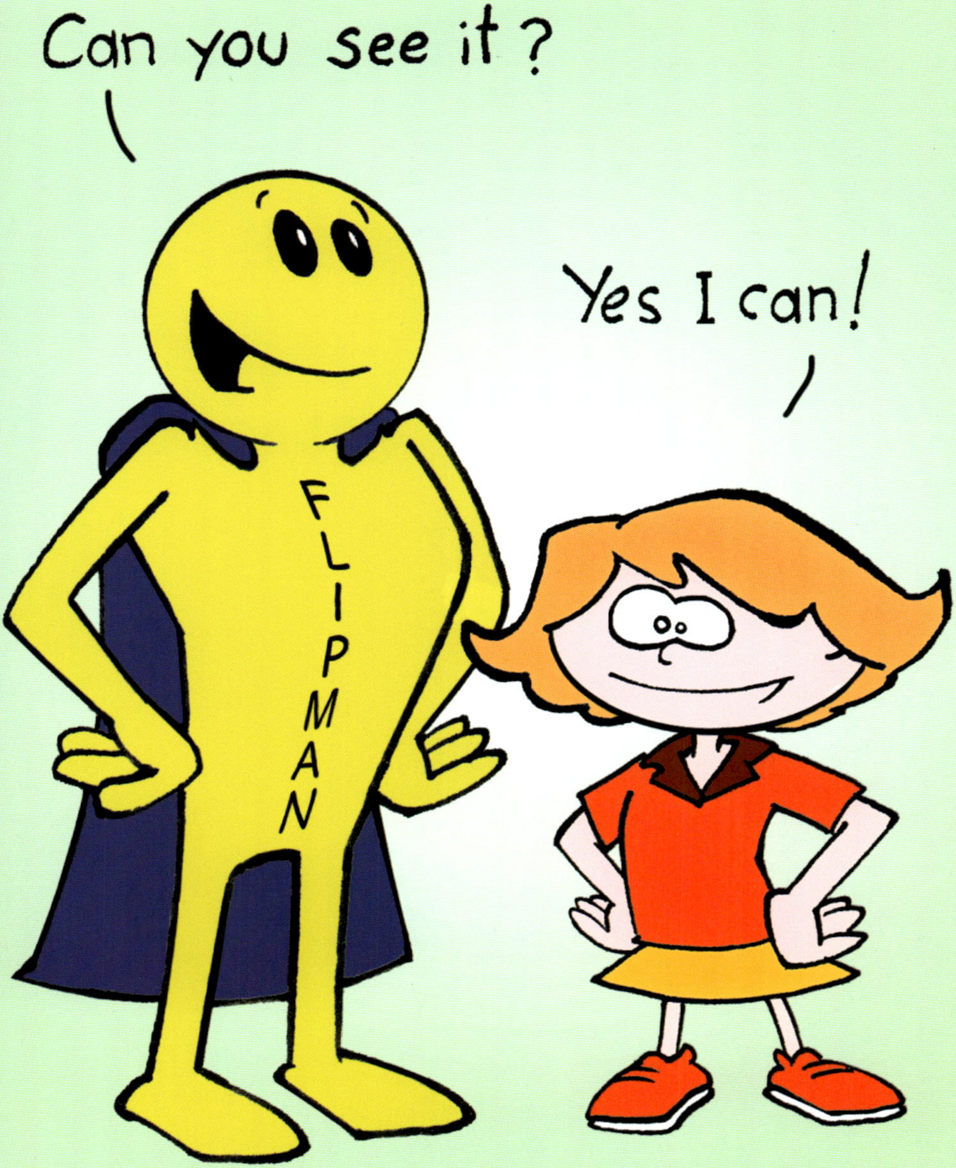
Can you see it?
Yes I can!
FLIPMAN

"Can you **HEAR** what you're saying to yourself when you're happy, healthy and positive, Chloe?"

"Yes I can, Flipman! I am saying:

I AM happy, healthy and positive!

I AM happy, healthy and positive!

I AM happy, healthy and positive!" said Chloe in a big, loud, happy voice.

Flipman was so proud of Chloe.

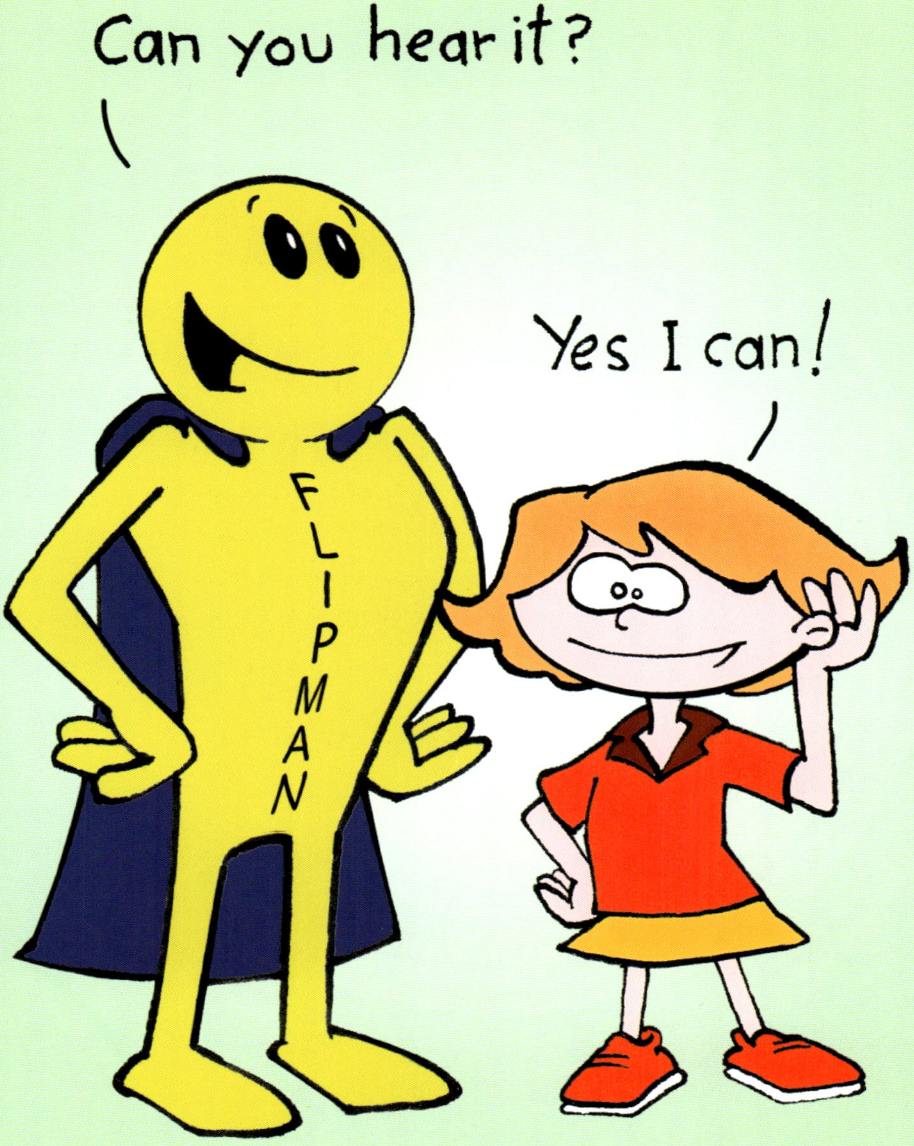
Can you hear it?
Yes I can!
FLIPMAN

"Can you use your imagination to FEEL how you will feel when you're happy, healthy and positive Chloe?"

"YES I CAN, Flipman!" said Chloe, getting more and more excited.

"It sounds like you're becoming a real FLIPGIRL Chloe," said Flipman.

"YAY!" Chloe laughed out loud as she jumped into the air.

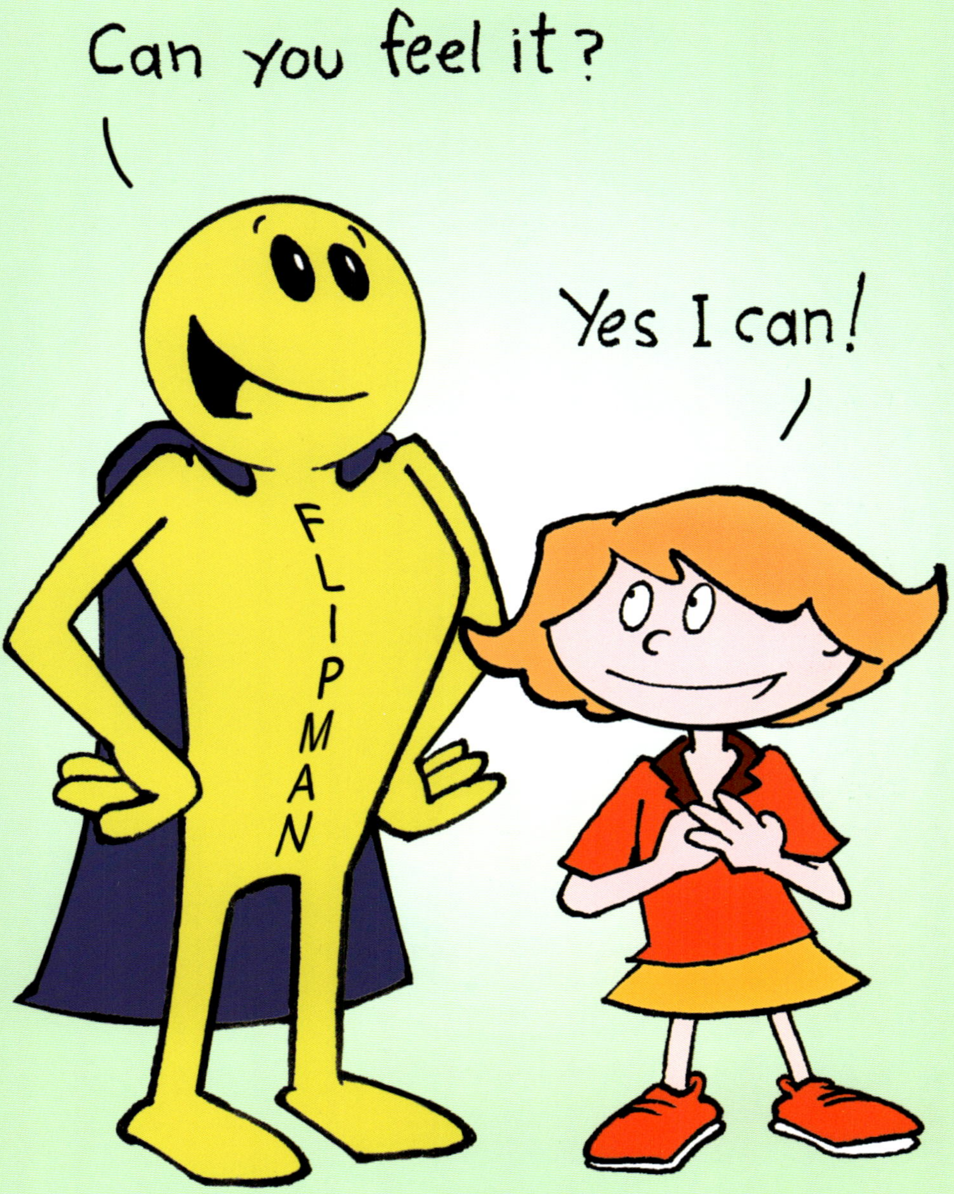
Can you feel it?
Yes I can!
FLIPMAN

"Can you remember what you **DO** when you are happy, healthy and positive, Chloe?"

"YES I CAN, Flipman!" said Chloe, with the biggest grin on her face. "I eat well, exercise, think positive thoughts and look after myself!" said Chloe confidently.

Chloe, you are so clever. Just remember the Flipman way is, SEE IT, SAY IT, FEEL IT, DO IT!" said Flipman.

SEE IT! Make a picture.

SAY IT! Say the words.

FEEL IT! Make a feeling.

DO IT! Do the actions.

"Oh Flipman, thank you so much. I feel great now that I know how to make myself feel better," said Chloe as she gave Flipman a great big hug goodbye. "I'll see you at the park when I'm better, Flipman!" she yelled out, as she watched Flipman meet up with Freddie and leave.

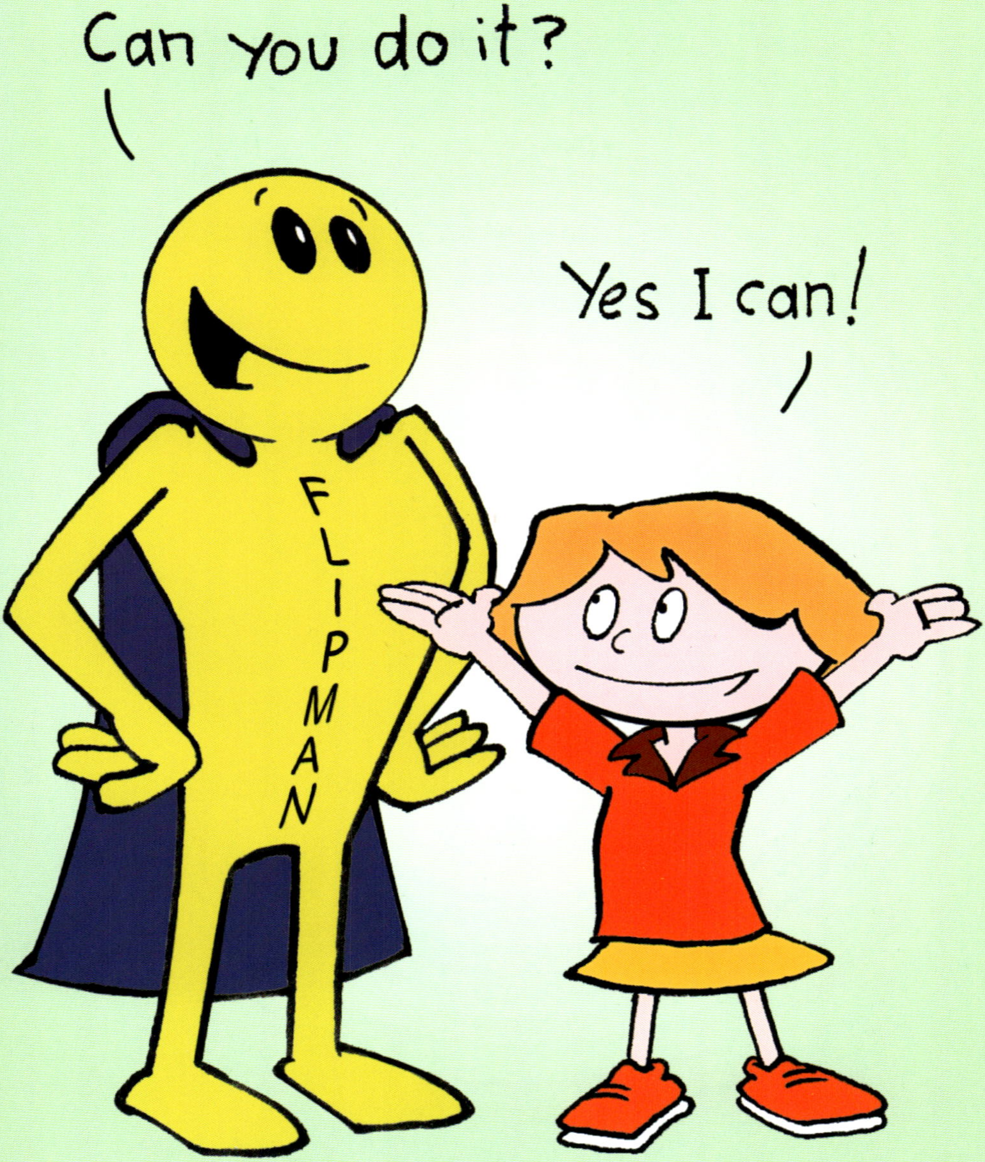
Can you do it?
Yes I can!
FLIPMAN

Chapter 5

A few months later Flipman was at the park again. His smile went even wider across his face as a happy, healthy, positive young girl ran up to him.

"Hi Flipman, I said I would see you at the park and here I am. The doctors say that I am in remission, which means that all the cancer cells have gone, but I like to say that I am 100% healthy, happy and positive!

"Now does that sound like a super FLIPGIRL to you, Flipman?" exclaimed Chloe looking very proud of herself.

"It sure does Chloe. WOW! I am so happy to see you looking so wonderful. You are such an inspiration," beamed Flipman.

"Flipman, I have learnt so many great things about looking after my body that I think all children could benefit from," said Chloe enthusiastically.

54

"That's fantastic Chloe! What are they?" asked Flipman.

"Well, the main thing we have to do is eat lots and lots of fresh fruit and vegetables every day. It's like putting really good fuel into our body, which helps our body fight disease. Exercise also helps our organs to be fit and healthy which makes them stronger too. I also learnt that the sun is great for us in small doses so if we are going to be spending lots of time outdoors especially at the beach, we should make sure that we do 3 things:

Number 1, put on some sunscreen.

Number 2, put on a shirt and...

Number 3, pop on a hat."

"WOW! Chloe, that is really helpful advice. Thank you so much. I'm sure there are lots of kids who will want to learn from you," said Flipman.

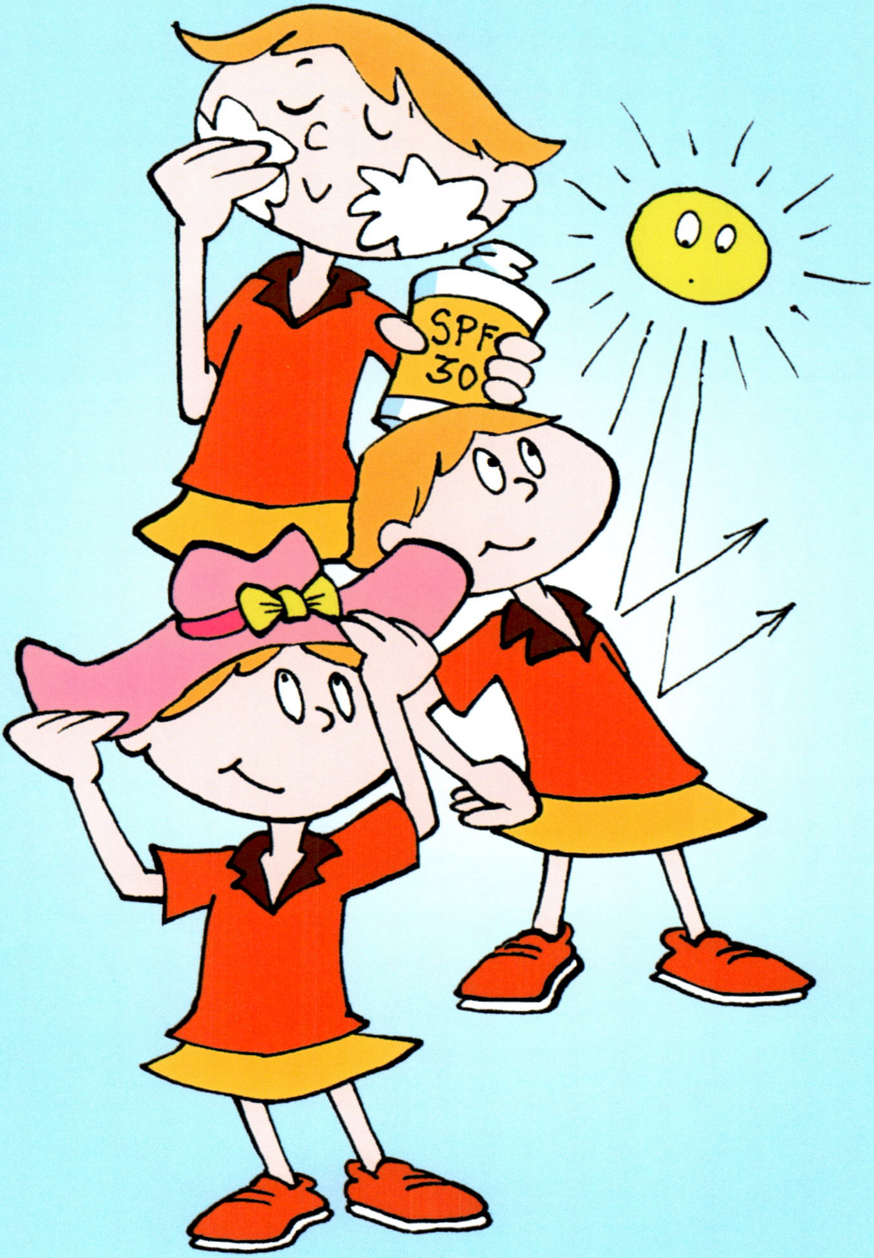
SPF
30

"Well, you'll have to excuse me, Flipman, because I'm off to help as many other kids as I can learn how to live a healthy, happy life," said Chloe as she skipped off down the path.

As Flipman waved goodbye to Chloe he also noticed Freddie skating down the path toward him.

"Hey Freddie! How's it going, man?" asked Flipman.

"Flipman! It's so great to see you," said Freddie.

"I have been a bit sad recently because my Grandpa passed away a few weeks ago.

"My entire family was with him and everyone was crying.

58

"I felt really scared but I remembered you telling me how important it was to feel all of our feelings and if I felt like crying, to cry and cry and cry till I had no more 'cry' left.

"I did that, which helped me feel a lot better. There were lots of people at the funeral and everyone said so many great things about him. I was very proud to have him as my Grandpa. I had lots of fun times with Grandpa and now I have lots of great memories.

"I still feel really sad at times but that just reminds me that I had a very special Grandpa who I will remember forever," said Freddie with a tear in his eye.

"Oh Freddie, that is so sad that your Grandpa passed away. I am really proud of how you have allowed yourself to feel all of your sadness. You were very close to him and I am sure this has been a really challenging time for you," said Flipman.

60

Chapter 6

"It can be a difficult time when we or anyone we love gets sick. At the moment we don't know why some people get better from cancer and others don't.

"So the best thing all of us can do is aim to live a healthy, happy and positive life. What we eat, how we exercise, how much fun we have and what we think, all help us to live a healthy life.

"Being a Flipman means living each day to its fullest and appreciating each moment we have.

"Thank you Freddie and Chloe for helping us all learn how to let our Flipman shine through, even if our life is challenging.

"Make it a great life, everyone, by looking after your body. Eat lots of healthy food, drink lots of water, get lots of exercise and protect yourself from the sun."

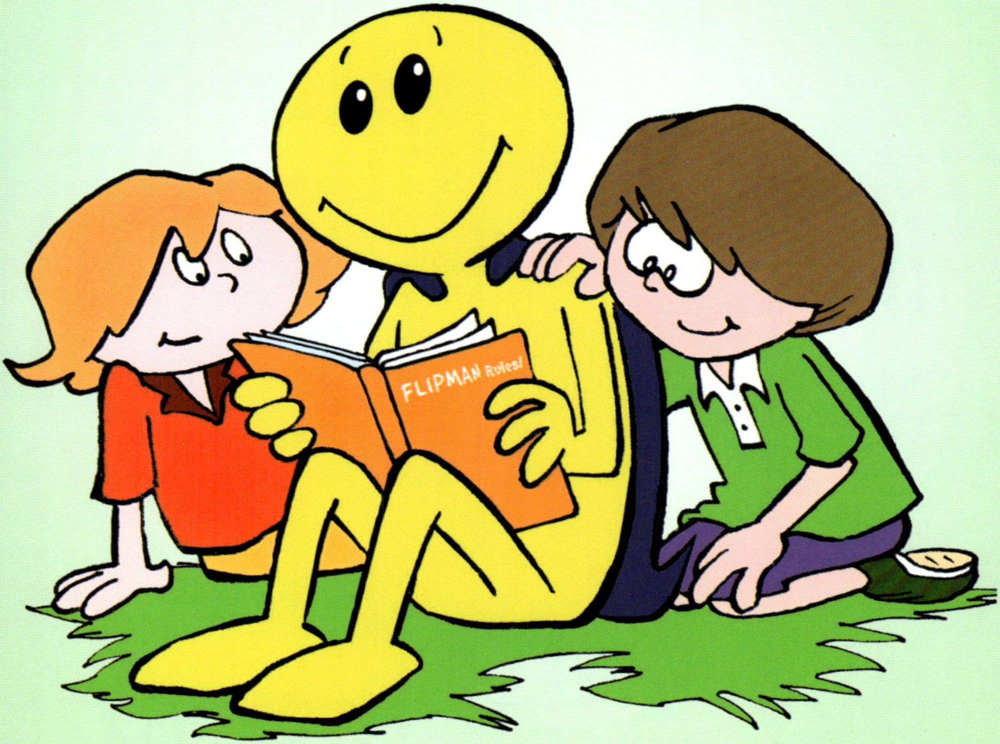
FLIPMAN Rules!

So ...
Let's DO Well!

GO Flipman!

About the Author

Terry Hawkins (CSP) is an award-winning educator, best selling author, successful businesswoman, in-demand speaker and loving mother. Her passion for giving people the tools to take ownership of their life is no more prevalent than in her adorable Flipman Rules! children's series.

This simple, down-to-earth string of beautifully designed books will give children a powerful support mechanism for life. Help them discover the positive brilliance of FLIPMAN® and the dangers and sadness associated with PITMAN® through this incredible series.

Other books by Terry Hawkins:

Books for Adults:
WHY WAIT TO BE GREAT? It's Either Now or Too late
Secrets of Inspiring Women EXPOSED (contributor)
The Power of More Than One (contributor)
20/20 A Fresh Look at Business Growth (contributor)

Books for Children:
Flipman Rules! Let's DO Healthy
Flipman Rules! Let's DO Happy
Flipman Rules! Let's DO Love
Flipman Rules! Let's DO Ability
Flipman Rules! Let's DO Well

For more information on Terry or her other products, visit www.terryhawkins.com

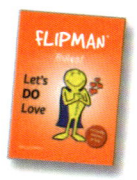

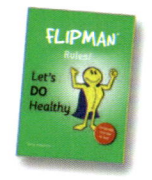

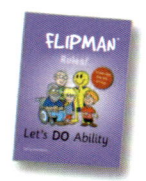

optus yes

At Optus, we care for our community and we are committed to making a meaningful difference through our partnerships with a range of charities and community organisations.

As an employer of over 9,000 people, we all know someone who has been touched by cancer either directly or indirectly. That's why we have been a proud supporter of Tour de Cure since 2009, helping bring messages of cancer awareness, prevention and support to communities across Australia.

Optus continues to support Tour de Cure in a variety of ways such as; using our network to enable the communications along the route, encouraging our people and our Optus stores to get involved - either through fundraising or participating in the ride to help raise the much needed funds to support those affected by cancer.

We know that together we can make a positive impact in the community and make a lasting difference.

For more information about how Optus is supporting the community visit:
www.optus.com.au/corporateresponsibility

LEXUS

No one disease elicits as much fear, emotion and compassion as cancer.

Likewise, the prospect of putting your own health and well-being on the line to cycle long distances visiting numerous communities along the way to raise funds for cancer and cancer related charities is a goal that made us at Lexus take notice.

Such a hefty goal requires a belief in what you are doing is for the greater good, and this is exactly the spirit that is embodied in the Tour de Cure team.

This goal and the people involved in the tour were all the motivation Lexus Australia needed to support Tour de Cure as it travels the road towards a cure for cancer.

Together, Tour de Cure and Lexus have been on a journey covering over 21,000 kilometres, raising in excess of $16million, promoting awareness towards cancer prevention and funding vital research, support and prevention projects.

The tour brings together like-minded people with one goal, to educate and inspire others about cancer, its impact, the choices we can make today and importantly funding research into finding a cure.

Lexus, a founding Partner and proud supporter since 2007 wishes the team safe travels as they embark on their next exciting journey.

Good luck team!

Woolworths Limited

With 1 in 2 men and 1 in 3 women likely to develop cancer in their lives, this disease will touch the people in the communities we serve and undoubtedly our employees. Whether it is somebody they know, a family member or sadly themselves, "cancer" will deeply impact all those that it touches.

As an employer of more than 190,000 employees, Woolworths is committed to the health and wellbeing of our people. With a third of all cancers preventable through lifestyle choices, Woolworths encourages our employees to live healthy lifestyles

With 28.4 million customers shopping with us each week we also believe it is important to make healthier options easier.

We applaud Tour de Cure's efforts to put an end to cancer. Woolworths is proud to support and assist in Tour de Cure's endeavours to fund vital cancer research, support and prevention projects and to finding a cure for cancer.

NOTES:

NOTES:

NOTES:

NOTES: